P9-AGO-576

The
BabeRuth
BALLET SCHOOL

For Ashley, who always wants to pitch.

A FIREFLY BOOK

Copyright © 1996 Tim Shortt

All rights reserved. The use of any part of this publication, reproduced, transmitted in any form or by any means, electronic, mechanical, photocopying, recording or otherwise, or stored in a retrieval system, without the prior consent of the publisher, is an infringement of the copyright law and is forbidden.

Cataloguing-in-Publication Data

Shortt, Tim
The Babe Ruth ballet school

ISBN 1-55209-030-2

1. Ruth, Babe. 1895-1948 - Juvenile literature.
2. Archer, Issy - Juvenile literature. 3. Baseball players - United States - Biography - Juvenile literature. I. Title.

GV865.A1S56 1996   j796.357'092'273   C96-930941-4

Published by
Firefly Books Ltd.
3680 Victoria Park Avenue
Willowdale, Ontario
Canada M2H 3K1

Published in the U.S. by
Firefly Books (U.S.) Inc.
P.O. Box 1338, Ellicott Station
Buffalo, New York 14205
U.S.A.

Design: Fortunato Aglialoro
Falcom Design & Communications Inc.

BALLET SCHOOL

Text and Illustrations by
Tim Shortt

FIREFLY BOOKS

The last 9-year-old girl to play Big League baseball was Issy Archer of the 1923 New York Yankees. Her pitches made the best batters swing like Little Leaguers.

At first, other players didn't respect her pitching.

Ty Cobb didn't. Issy struck him out. Tris Speaker didn't. Issy dusted him off. Goose Goslin didn't. Issy sent him packing.

Issy Archer didn't throw hard. She didn't throw fast. She threw spitballs. Soaking, sopping-wet spitballs. The sports reporters said, "Wear your snorkel and flippers when Issy's on the mound."

After games, Issy chummed around with Babe Ruth, her Yankee teammate and best friend. Sometimes they would go to the Bronx Zoo. Issy liked the lions. Babe liked the penguins. Or they would go to Coney Island, where they liked to crash bumper cars and eat cotton candy. Sometimes Issy's mother would invite Babe to supper in the apartment above the sheet-music and radio store, where Issy lived with her mother and her grandmother. "Hello, kid, how are you?" Babe would always say to Issy's grandmother.

Issy and Babe liked to ask each other baseball questions.

"Who scored 177 runs in 1921?" asked Issy.

"Babe Ruth," answered Babe. "Who drank the most Fizzy Pink Sodas in one sitting?"

"Babe Ruth," answered Issy. "Who is the all-time home-run hitter, with 59 home runs?"

"Babe Ruth. New York Yankees, 1921," answered Babe. "Who broke all records at last year's All-You-Can-Eat Chili-Dog Festival?" asked Babe.

"Babe Ruth," answered Issy. "Who pitched 29⅔ straight scoreless innings in World Series play?"

"Babe Ruth. Boston Red Sox, 1916 and 1918," answered Babe.

6

Issy had a secret that she couldn't tell Babe. The thing she loved most, even better than baseball, was dancing. From the roof of her building, Issy could hear her upstairs neighbor, Mr. Miller, play his violin. There, every evening under the stars and the moonlight, she would dance to his melodies. "Someday," Issy thought, "I'll dance in the great halls of Europe, and all the cultured people of Paris, Rome and Vienna will be enchanted by my artistry."

Issy would dance until her mother or her grandmother called, "Bedtime, Issy. You have a big game to pitch tomorrow." Issy never told Babe about her dancing. He was her very best friend, but she was afraid he might laugh at her.

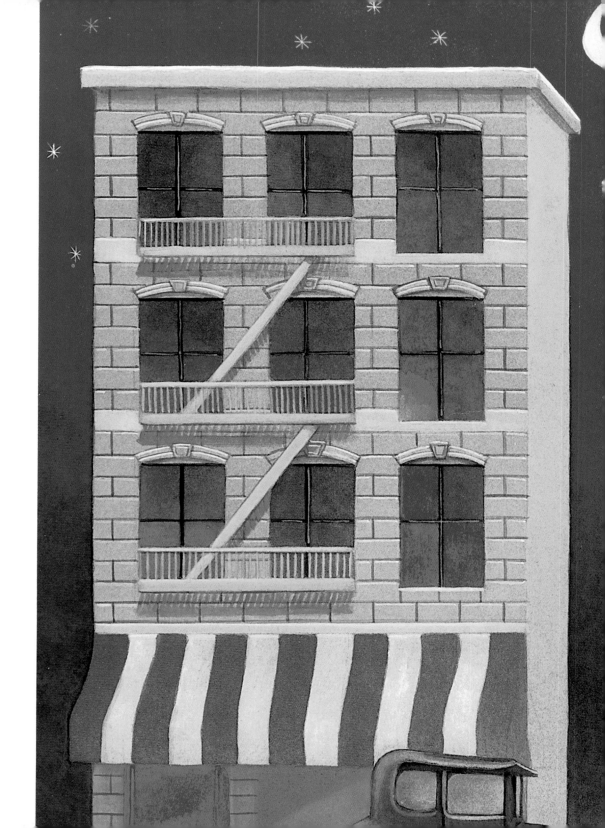

One day, after Issy had just pitched the Yankees to a 6-1 win over the Cleveland Indians, Babe carried two Fizzy Pink Sodas and a big box of peanut brittle to her locker. But ahead, he saw Issy already leaving, carrying a small suitcase. "Hi ya, Babe," yelled Issy. "Look, gotta go. Can't wait around. See you later. That was some big home run you hit today, Babe." She waved as she left, then she was gone.

Babe guzzled the second Fizzy Pink Soda. He dug his big, big hand into the peanut brittle. "More for me," he said to himself.

Issy Archer was always busy now. When the All-Clown Circus came to town, Issy Archer couldn't go. When the Gooey Sticky Saltwater Taffy Pull was held, Issy Archer was unavailable. When the new Four Windmill MiniGolf opened, Issy Archer was just too busy.

Babe often chased after her. "Where are you going?" he asked. "What's so important? What's in the suitcase? Why can't I come too?"

When Issy Archer couldn't go to the All-You-Can-Eat Chili-Dog Festival, Babe Ruth said he would find a new friend. "You never want to do any fun stuff anymore," he said. "We're supposed to be teammates, Issy Archer. Best buddies. You won't even tell me where you're going every day that's just so gosh-darn important."

It was the third inning of a game against the St. Louis Browns. The Yankees were at bat. They were leading 3-0.

"Not to some Chili-Dog Festival," said Issy. "Somewhere thick-headed baseball players wouldn't understand. Somewhere sophisticated."

"La-di-da," said Babe. "Well, kid, Wally Pipp isn't too sophisticated to go to an All-You-Can-Eat Chili-Dog Festival with Babe Ruth." He crossed his arms and moved to sit beside Wally Pipp, the Yankee's first baseman.

Issy Archer allowed the Browns to score nine runs in the next inning. She was taken out of the game. It was the worst game she had ever pitched.

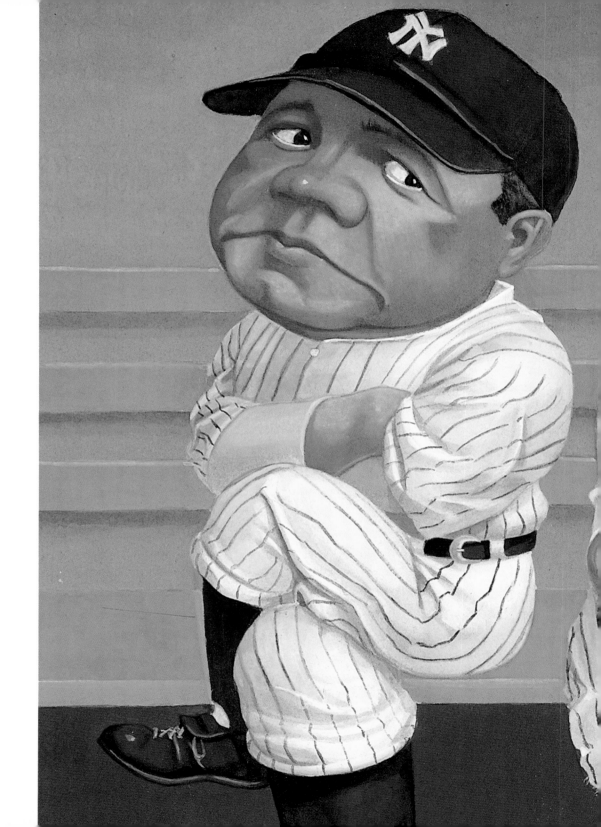

The Browns were now leading the Yankees 9-8.

"Since you can't live without knowing, I'm dancing," said Issy. "I go to dance classes."

"Dancing? But Issy, dancing's so girlish," said Babe.

"I'm a girl, Babe," said Issy.

Babe picked up a bat. He walked to the on-deck circle. He took some big home-run practice swings. Then he walked back to Issy. "Yeah, I know," said Babe. "But you're kind of a fellow, right?"

"I'm a girl, Babe," said Issy Archer.

"Dancing," said Babe, shaking his head. "Fellas, you hear that? Issy's a dancer. Can you believe that, a dancer?"

"What's wrong with dancing?" said Aaron Ward.

"My wife's a dancer," said Silent Bob Meusal.

"I bet you're a great dancer, Issy," said Schoolboy Hoyt. Wally Schang picked his banjo off the bat rack, and Herb Pennock pulled out his harmonica. Issy and Bullet Joe Bush danced the fox-trot across the dugout.

Babe walked to bat, shaking his head. He struck out. The Yankees lost the game.

Babe met Issy as she was leaving. "I've been talking to some guys about doing a vaudeville show in the off-season," he said. "And this big Hollywood producer might want to do a moving picture with me. So I'm thinking if I can come to your classes, dancing would be good training. You know, for the stage and all."

"I think it would be, Babe," said Issy. "After, we'll go to the Chili-Dog Festival. You'll be ready for a dozen dogs by then, Babe."

"A dozen? Two dozen, easy," said Babe.

"A new record for Babe Ruth," said Issy Archer.

Babe Ruth quickly became one of Miss Ilona's favorite students. Teacher's pet, the other dancers called him.

At the ballpark, Babe was slugging more home runs than ever. When he didn't hit a homer, he hit a double or a triple.

The sports reporters asked why his hitting was unstoppable.

"Fellas," said Babe Ruth, "you might think me funny, but I credit my dance lessons. The dance, see, helps my balance and my movement."

"But, Babe, dancing's so girlish," said the sports reporters.

"Fellas," said Babe Ruth, "I'm an athlete, and dancing is athletic."

16

A few days later, the now famous photo-graph of Babe Ruth in dance tights, sur-rounded by Issy Archer and all the other dancers of Miss Ilona's Dance Academy, was taken. You have probably seen it. It's a very famous picture.

Soon, all of New York wanted to see Babe Ruth dance. Large crowds gathered outside Miss Ilona's Dance Academy.

Then Issy announced her retirement from professional baseball. "When a person turns 10, she needs to consider her future," said Issy Archer. "I have chosen to dedicate myself to a dance career." Issy would pitch her last game three games later. Afterward, as a tribute to Issy, Miss Ilona's Dance Academy would dance a ballet in Yankee Stadium. The line to buy tickets circled the ballpark three times.

Babe got nervous.

Then Babe missed the game against the Washington Senators. He missed the game against the Philadelphia Athletics. The sports reporters began to worry. They heard rumors that Babe was sick with a bellyache. They feared he wouldn't recover in time to dance the ballet. Issy visited Babe. His room was littered with Fizzy Pink Soda bottles and Cracker Jack boxes. He was eating chocolate cake.

"Your illness hasn't crippled your appetite," said Issy.

"It only hurts when I stop eating," said Babe.

"You'll miss my final game," said Issy.

"Shame. It's a shame," said Babe.

"You don't want to dance, do you?" asked Issy.

"I'm a home-run hitter, not a dancer," said Babe.

"The fans will love you anyway, Babe. They always do. You know that," said Issy. "Babe Ruth doesn't hide. I want you at my game."

Then she left.

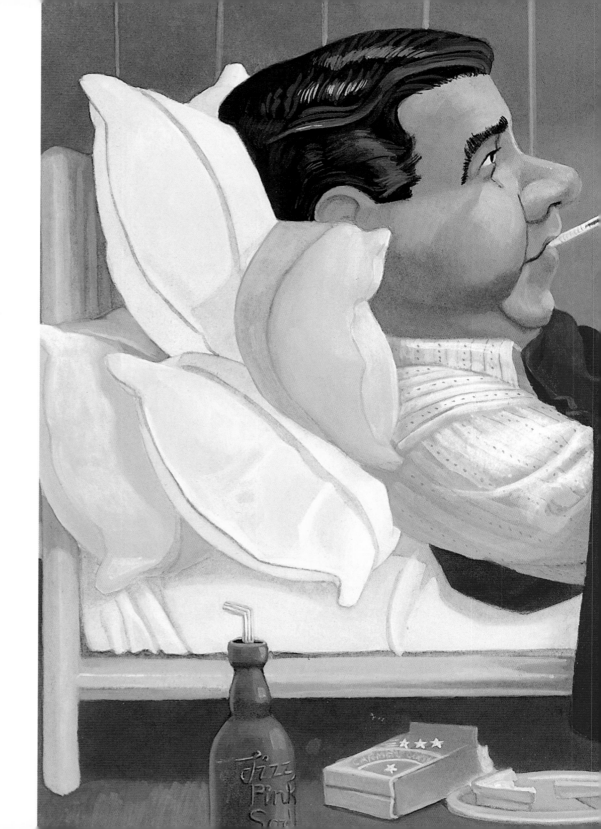

This would be Issy Archer's final game. She was given a 10-minute standing ovation. When the name Babe Ruth was announced, the crowd hushed, leaned forward and watched the Yankee dugout. Was Babe Ruth here? Would he be able to play? Babe wobbled weakly out of the dugout wearing an old bathrobe and carrying an ice pack on his head. He was bent over, clutching his stomach with both hands. The crowd applauded politely but was disappointed when it saw that he was too sick to perform.

Issy was unhittable. Babe moaned and groaned and kept the batboy hustling into the stands for Fizzy Pink Sodas and Eskimo Pies.

In the bottom of the fifth, two Detroit Tiger players, Ty Cobb and Topper Rigney, waltzed together past the Yankee bench. "You dance divinely, Babe," said Rigney.

"I bet you say that to all the girls," said Cobb.

When Cobb made two errors next inning, Babe jumped quickly out of the dugout. "Pretty lousy footwork, Cobb," said Babe. "May I suggest that dance lessons might do you some good?" Then, seeing everyone watching him, Babe grabbed his stomach. "Oh, my poor tummy," said Babe.

Issy Archer pitched a perfect game through nine innings. Not a single Tiger reached base.

But the Yankees were also unable to score. When they took their last at bat, the score was 0-0. Then Jumping Joe Dugan hit a ground out. Whitey Witt struck out. The Yankees had one last chance to win the game.

"Win this game, Babe," said Issy Archer. She handed him his bat.

"Win it for Issy," said the other Yankees.

Babe finished his hotdog. He set down his Fizzy Pink Soda. He removed his ice pack.

"Win the game for Issy, Babe," shouted the crowd.

"Sure, kid, I'll sock one out for you," said Babe.

He did. He hit the first pitch over the center-field fence. The Yankees won the game!

Babe danced to first base. He leapt gracefully into second. He pirouetted to third. He came home on the tips of his toes.

At home plate, Babe lifted Issy high into the sky. Together, they danced over the pitcher's mound, over second base and into center field. Miss Ilona's dancers and the rest of the Yankees followed.

The biggest ever Yankee Stadium crowd, 72,000 people, stood and danced and cheered for Babe Ruth and Issy Archer.

The famous writer Ernest Hemingway once told a story of his days in Paris. In a park beside the Eiffel Tower, Ernest and some reporters from the *International Herald Tribune* played a game of baseball against a team of *petites filles*.

"They always beat us," said Ernest. "These little French girls from a dance school. *Le Corps de Ballet de Babe Ruth*, we called them. They had an American teacher, Miss Isabella. And I swear, they were pitching spitballs."

Printed in Canada